Geiszel

A Chapter Book by

Geiszel Godoy

Illustrations by Huan Lim

Published by

Contact

www.blacksandsentertainment.com

Geiszel@blacksandsentertainment.com

Instagram: Instagram.com/Mori_Adventures

Facebook:
https://www.Facebook.com/MoriAdventures

This book or parts thereof may not be reproduced in any form, stored in a retrieval system, or transmitted in any form by any means—electronic, mechanical, photocopy, recording, or otherwise—without prior written permission of the publisher, except as provided by US copyright law.

Copyright © 2018 by Geiszel Godoy
All rights reserved.
ISBN 13: 9780999473443
ISBN 10: 0999473441

Contents

1) HOME 1

2) NEXT STOP, BRAZIL! 5

3) THE REDEEMER 12

4) UP IN THE MOUNTAINS 17

5) NATIONAL MUSEUM PT. 1 25

6) NATIONAL MUSEUM PT. 2 33

7) EXCURSION IN THE AMAZON 39

8) FESTIVAL 47

9) A NIGHT TO REMEMBER 53

This book is dedicated to my lovely family and Kickstarter fans around the world. Thank you all for your support!

Brazilian Culture Exchange

HOME

"Mom, wake up!" I exclaimed, running over to her. "I just had the best dream ever!"

"What did you dream of, Mori?" replied Mom.

"I dreamed that we were in Brazil, and we were playing in the Amazon with the animals!"

"Mori, your dream will come true in less than a week," said Mom, putting a smile on our faces. "We will be going to Brazil on a family vacation."

"That's right, son," Dad added. "We are heading to the largest African Diaspora in the world."

Valencia asked, "What's an African Diaspora, Dad?"

"An African Diaspora is a community that developed from the forced movement of the African people by colonial powers a long, long time ago."

"Yay! I can't wait to see all the animals," she replied happily.

I questioned, "So, Dad… what kind of things can we do in Brazil?"

"Well son, apart from the Amazon and thousands of wonderful animals, Brazil has amazing beaches, carnivals, amazing statues like *Christ the Redeemer*, and beautiful architecture." said Dad.

My little sister and I jumped up and down with glee as we thought about all the fun things we were going to do on our trip.

"I'm going to eat a lot of cakes and sweets!" exclaimed Valencia.

"I'm going to be one with nature!" I screamed, and my little sister started laughing out loud as I hit my chest like king gorillas do.

A little later, I started running around, just like a jaguar. Valencia and I played chase, and we imitated our favorite animals. She spread her arms in the air like a bird. Meanwhile, Mom and Dad were planning for our vacation.

The next day, we started to pack for our adventurous trip to Brazil. Valencia called out to me in the middle of packing.

"Yes?" I replied.

"Do you want to pack the dogs in your suitcase or mine?"

"Valencia, we can't take Black and Brown with us by

putting them inside the suitcase!" I laughed at her funny question.

"But I will miss them..." Valencia pouted as we resumed stuffing important things into our luggage.

"The dogs are not allowed to travel with us, little sis." I said. "And you could hurt Black and Brown by putting them inside!"

"But..."

"Okay kids, let's focus on packing now," answered Mom. "And Mori, please remind me to bring the new camera with us so that we can take pictures there."

"Dad, how long is the flight to Brazil?" I asked.

"The flight will last for eight hours, son," replied Dad with a smile.

On the day before our flight, Dad woke up to the fresh aroma of Mom cooking pancakes and scrambled eggs in the kitchen. As soon as I heard Mom's voice calling us for breakfast, I jumped out of bed as quickly as I could, excited to tell all of our friends and neighbors that we're flying to Brazil tomorrow!

"Yippeeee!" shouted Valencia.

"Mori and Valencia, you guys need to go to bed on time tonight because we have a long flight ahead of us," reminded Mom.

Dad added, "That's right, kids," giving Valencia and I some cookies after we finished assisting Mom in washing and drying the dishes.

As the dawn appeared, Mom began to put us in bed. Of course, Valencia and I said our prayers first before going to sleep. Mom kissed our foreheads before wishing us a good night.

We were awakened from our sleep by Black and Brown's loud barking. As Mom and Dad got up from bed, they realized that the alarm they had set last night didn't sound off at the appropriate time.

Brazilian Culture Exchange

NEXT STOP, BRAZIL!

"Oh no, it's five a.m.!" exclaimed Mom as she jumped out of bed. "We were all supposed to get up at four a.m."

Dad answered, "Well, to look at it in a positive way... thank goodness our dogs woke us up with their loud barking, or it could have been worse."

"Okay, everyone! Let us hurry and get to the airport in time for our flight!" said Mom, dragging Valencia and I out of bed.

Later on, Mom and Dad dropped Black and Brown off with the neighbor so they could be taken care of while we were in Brazil. The people living next door were more than happy to take care of Black and Brown. Valencia and I dropped by to say thank you for their kindness before heading to the car.

After a short drive, our family arrived at the Atlanta International Airport. We were all filled with so much excitement. In fact, I think I was too excited for my own good. I had to ask Dad to accompany me to the restroom.

"Dad, I have to go pee."

"Be quick! We only have ten more minutes before

we board the plane," said Mom.

"Let's run!"

Dad and I quickly ran to the restroom. After five minutes, we went back to Mom and Valencia who were already getting ready to board the plane.

"Calling all passengers…"

"Brazil, here we come!"

"Yes! That's right, kids!" Dad grinned in excitement as we all walked towards the boarding gate.

We finally boarded the plane. As it took off, Dad looked at Mom, gave her a kiss, and said that we were finally taking our dream vacation after a long wait.

During our eight-and-a-half-hour flight, Dad went over the itinerary of the different places that he and Mom were bringing us to.

"Mom, please take us to the kids' carnival!" I pleaded. "Oh! And, and the Amazon to see all the animals!"

"Yes!" replied Valencia. "Please take us there!"

"Alright, children. Your Dad and I will take you to

all of those places," agreed Mom, pinching my cheeks.

"Dad wants to visit all the famous steakhouses in Brazil!" exclaimed Dad, making Valencia and I laugh in our seats. "Brazil is known for their endless steaks. I can't believe a country like that even exists."

I added, "I want steak too!"

"I don't like steak! It's blooooody!" said Valencia while raising her hands in the air and making random gestures.

"You're all too noisy, you will disturb the other passengers!" reminded Mom. After making sure that we were calm enough to resume the conversation, she continued.

"Dad, you should stick to your diet regardless of where we go. If you don't take care of your health, Mori, Valencia, and I will be worried."

"Hmph," he grumbled, "but I can still have one or two pieces of steak."

Mom added, "Just promise you won't go on a steak marathon like you said earlier…"

Dad frowned, and Mom joked that he looked like

me when I complain about my favorite cartoon series ending. Dad didn't want to talk about our itinerary because of that conversation with Mom and the fact that he can't go on a "steak marathon," so he just shared some very interesting information about Brazil with me and Valencia instead.

"Kids, did you know that Brazil is the fifth largest country in the whole world? Similarly, it is home to the Amazon River, which is the second longest river on the planet."

"That's amazing!" Valencia and I screamed in unison.

After a few hours, we finally landed in Rio De Janeiro, Brazil. The locals greeted us with a smile. They wore clothes with vibrant colors, which were appropriate for the tropical setting.

I couldn't help but exclaim, "Wow, this place is very different from our hometown!"

As soon as we arrived, we went straight to the hotel where we were staying, the Rio Othon Palace. This hotel was just by the Copacabana Beach in Rio De Janeiro, one of the most famous beaches in the world.

Mom gasped, "This is breathtaking!"

Entering our suite, Mom and Dad set our luggage aside while Valencia and I jumped on the big, soft bed. The whole room was spacious and we had an amazing view of the city from the huge windows!

A few minutes later, we all took turns taking a shower to refresh ourselves for a great adventure ahead. I put on my swimwear, and some sunblock to keep my skin protected.

"Okay kids, since we have everything settled... let's head to the beach!" said Dad, with excitement written all over his face.

Mom added, "It's awesome to have our hotel by the beach. We can go swimming and relax by the shore as much as we want."

As soon as our family reached the seaside, my little sister and I immediately ran through the sand. Mom and Dad decided to walk along the beach and explore the wonderful views.

A few moments later, Valencia and I were making sand castles while Mom and Dad sat down beside us, and watched the sky painted in orange and yellow as the sun came down. We took a few pictures of our sandcastle and the beautiful sunset with Dad's new camera. Valencia and I took some selfies and when it was already getting dark, we headed back to the hotel to get some rest.

The next day, we took a tour of Mount Corcovado to see the wonderful statue of *Christ the Redeemer*! The people in Brazil totally respect this statue and most of them, especially the Christians, see Christ as the Savior of the world.

Geiszel Godoy

THE REDEEMER

"Mori, wake up now," whispered Mom as she gently tapped my shoulder. "We're almost there."

"..."

"Mom, where are we again?" asked Valencia.

Mom answered, "We're heading to the top of Mount Corcovado, dear."

"Mount Avocado? Is it tasty?"

Dad laughs inside the car, and I wake up from a short nap. Mom tells Valencia that we are heading to the top of Mount Corcovado, not Mount Avocado.

Mom says that the mountain stands 2,310 feet tall, and that the largest sculpture in the world, *Christ the Redeemer*, can be viewed at the very top.

We'll be able to see the whole view of Rio de Janeiro from there, including the surrounding mountains, the ocean, the forests and even the large buildings in the city.

"We're here!"

"Yay!" cheered my little sister and I.

My little sister and I get out of the van, and Mom holds our hands. Dad follows behind us, making sure that nobody is left behind.

"Wow!"

Right before us was Papa Jesus' huge statue. It shone brightly under the sunlight. I think I hurt my neck a little from looking up too much because it was so high!

Mom says that Papa Jesus' statue stands at ninety-eight feet tall, but I think it is tall enough to touch the clouds.

While Dad was busy taking pictures of the big statue, Valencia and I walked around with Mom. We approached an old man who gave us a bright smile.

"It is wonderful, isn't it?" asked the old man. "This statue was built back in 1931, but it still stands tall up to this day."

He added, "The Roman church proposed that a statue of Jesus Christ be built on this mountain in 1921. Believe it or not, the construction started in 1926 and lasted for five years.

"This statue has been visited by Pope John Paul II in the past, and has been named as one of the New

Seven Wonders of the World."

"That is amazing!"

Mom continued talking to the wise old man while Valencia and I explored our surroundings.

She reminded us, "Don't go too far, children!

I exclaimed, "Little sis, look!"

We walked towards the railings, only to spot Hyacinth Macaws, the largest parrots in the world, emerging from the trees and into the sky.

"Mom! Why isn't Dad saying anything?"

Valencia pointed to Dad, who had a terrified look written all over his face.

"We're so high up off the ground…" answered Dad in a soft manner.

"Dad is afraid of heights!"

"I'm not afraid of heights!"

Mom smiled at Dad and told him not to be afraid, like me. She held his hand and soon after, we ran and gave him a warm hug.

Brazilian Culture Exchange

"We love you, Dad!"

"This is the best trip ever!"

Brazilian Culture Exchange

UP IN THE MOUNTAINS

After going to Corcovado Mountain yesterday, Valencia and I were very excited for our next destination. On the second day of the trip, our family prepared to take a tour of Sugarloaf Mountain.

With this in mind, we went down from our suite to the restaurant, just inside the hotel, so we could get our breakfast first before another day of adventure. We were greeted by the lovely smiles of the waiters and waitresses in the room and a Brazilian way of saying good morning:

"Bom dia!"

We found our seats and the waiter gave Mom and Dad the menu. They ordered a traditional Brazilian breakfast for us to try. Several minutes later, the food arrived and it looked super delicious. There was a wide variety to choose from.

"What is that?" I pointed at a bowl filled with purple-looking-mousse, causing the waiter to smile.

"What you have before you is our Traditional Brazilian Breakfast Set. This breakfast is most famous among tourists who wish to know more about our traditions, so we offer a wide variety of delicacies they might want to try," said the waiter.

"That is called Açaí Na Tigela or Brazilian Açaí Breakfast. Açaí are nutritious berries that grow on palm in Central and South America. They have a bright, sweet flavor and are very deep purple in color. We make it into a frozen puree, like a sorbet, topped with granola and guarana syrup. Guarana is a fruit from the Amazon that is thought to have many health benefits," he explained.

After giving it a taste, Mom was extremely satisfied with it, saying that if she had access to açaí berries back at home, she would make this sweet but nutritious breakfast for us every day. Dad asked the waiter about the other components of our traditional Brazilian breakfast, which he gladly explained.

"Here in Brazil, breakfast is not the biggest or most important meal of the day; we tend to eat a lighter breakfast. Coffee is a very important part of the Brazilian breakfast, and I highly recommend our very own special blend.

"On this side, we have skillet-toasted French bread rolls or pão na chapa which is a favorite, quick breakfast that is highly accessible to the masses in this area. Aside from acai na tigela, we also have cheese and meat, cake, cornmeal and manioc as options for a delicious breakfast."

"What's manioc?" I asked.

"Is it normal for Brazilians to have cake for breakfast?" asked Valencia.

"Manioc is a key staple in our cuisine. It is also known as *yuca and cassava*, which you might be more familiar with. On the other hand, having cake for breakfast is perfectly normal in Brazil, dear. I highly recommend cuca de banana which is a German-style banana coffee cake for breakfast. What you have in front of you right now is our chef's special orange cake."

"Wow! I want to live in Brazil forever!" exclaimed Valencia.

"You and your Dad would fit in here, Valencia. Unfortunately, you are not allowed to eat cakes and steaks all the time," reminded Mom.

"Awwww," said Valencia with a frown, causing Dad to laugh this time.

We thanked the waiter for a brief introduction before dining on the mouthwatering food in front of us. Similarly, we kept on talking while eating, and a few minutes later, I realized that Dad looked very nervous as we talked about Sugarloaf Mountain. I decided to ask him why.

"Dad, why do you look so nervous?"

"Son, you know I dislike heights… and now I have to do it again," replied Dad. "But for you, I will conquer my fear of heights."

"That's my Super Dad!" Valencia exclaimed out of nowhere, causing Mom to laugh.

My little sister and I gave Dad a big hug before going back to our seat to finish our sandwiches. After eating, we went back to our room to get prepared for our trip to Sugarloaf Mountain.

"Okay everyone, let's go and enjoy our time in Brazil!" said Mom as we left the hotel.

Dad, Mom, Valencia and I rode a taxi to Praia Vermelha or the Red Beach. There, we would be able to catch the cable car that will bring us to the top of Sugarloaf Mountain.

During the ride, Mom told us that Sugarloaf Mountain offers amazing views of Guanabara Bay and the whole city of Rio de Janeiro. It dates back to 600 million years ago, which is amazing!

Brazilian Culture Exchange

"Now, how ancient is that?" I replied.

Valencia added, "600 million years ago… were there any dinosaurs then?"

Dad was about to reply, but the taxi suddenly came to a stop.

"Okay guys, it's time to get into the cable car to go up the mountain," said Mom while we got out of the taxi.

"Dad, you should go first!" I stated, giving Dad the largest grin I could manage.

However, Mom gave me a serious look while saying, "Mori, leave your father alone. He is really brave for coming with us."

"But Mom, I was just kidding around!"

"Dad is a hero and I love him," said Valencia proudly.

Mom lined up to buy tickets for us. After that, our whole family lined up to ride the cable car. After a few minutes, we finally got settled into the cable car. It was a glass cable car that can transport 1,360 passengers per hour. More than thirty-seven million people have traveled in these cable cars for them to reach the top of Sugarloaf Mountain.

The first cable car brought us to Urca Mountain. During the ride, we were able to see Copacabana Beach and even *Christ the Redeemer* statue! It was amazing to see the statue from afar this time, after being up close to it yesterday. Next, we rode a second cable car to the top of Sugarloaf Mountain.

"Wow, this is impressive!" I exclaimed in excitement.

"Look, there's Sugarloaf Mountain!" Mom pointed out. Valencia asked a funny question right after, making all of us burst into laughter.

"Why are all of the mountains here named after tasty things? First, Avocado Mountain... and now we're going to Sugarloaf Mountain!"

"Valencia, it's Corcovado!" replied Dad, tears forming at the corners of his eyes from holding his laughter.

"It is named Sugarloaf Mountain because it resembles a sugarloaf, dear," explained Mom.

A few minutes later, we finally got to the top of Sugarloaf Mountain. Mom said the view is breathtaking, and I completely agree. We were 395 meters above the ground at the moment, and the seas looked amazing from up there! There are small islands all around the area, and the large buildings in the city looked as small as my toys at home.

"Dad, are you still nervous?"

"A little, son. But as long as you guys are enjoying it, Dad is happy," replied Dad as I held his hand.

We stood side by side, watching the wonderful view. Dad's fear started to disappear, and later on, he even told jokes to make us laugh. I am very happy to be here with Mom, Dad and Valencia, and I will never forget this trip, not ever!

Brazilian Culture Exchange

THE NATIONAL MUSEUM PT. 1

On the fourth day of our trip, Dad decided to take us to a well-known museum to learn more about Brazil, its history and its people. I asked him a question while we were watching television inside our hotel room.

"So Dad, can you tell me who the first people to live in Brazil were?"

"Mori, the Natives, also known as Brazilian Indians, were the first people to live in Brazil," answered Dad.

"Why are they called Indians if they are Brazilians?" I asked.

"Mori, the name Indian supposedly originated from Christopher Columbus, an Italian explorer, navigator and colonizer, who once thought that he had reached the East Indies when he didn't. He referred to the people in the lands he visited as 'indios' which is Spanish for Indian," he explained. "This is why we call them Brazilian Indians or just Indians, and this name is accepted and understood by a number of history enthusiasts."

After that, Dad shared a lot of information with me

about Brazil's history and I learned an abundant amount of knowledge from our conversation.

Dad told me that an explorer named Pedro Cabral, who was born in Portugal back in 1467, was the European explorer who landed in Brazil on April 22, 1500. He came from a noble family and was a member of the Royal Portuguese Court of King John and King Manuel I. Pedro Cabral only found Brazil by accident, as he was supposed to travel to India. On the way to India, he turned the direction of his ship towards the west and landed in Brazil instead.

Dad also said that sugarcanes were planted in Brazil back in the 1530s. Sugar has played an important role in Brazil's economic and social history. Brazil accounts for approximately twenty percent of global production and over forty percent of world exports. He added that Brazil is the leading producer of sugar and more than one hundred countries rely on Brazil for sugar.

However, this also led to imported slavery, with roughly forty percent of the estimated population of Rio de Janeiro being slaves in 1550. The slave trade in Brazil went on until it was formally stopped by the imperial family on May 13, 1888.

Brazilian Culture Exchange

"So Dad, since we live in the United States of America, does that mean that we get our sugar from Brazil too?" I had to ask Dad this question after everything that he shared with me.

"Actually Mori," replied Dad, "most of our sugar in the U.S. comes from Louisiana and Florida. A small percentage comes from Hawaii and Texas, however."

"Wow!" exclaimed Valencia. "I didn't know that."

"I love sugar!" Valencia and I shouted at the same time. "It is sooooo good!"

Mom joined us and said that Brazil's total population is about 211 million people. It is the largest country in South America.

"Alright kids, we need to head over to the museum now. We can watch your favorite show again later," reminded Mom. We immediately stood up and started preparing for another exciting trip.

"Yay! Let's go to the museum!" I replied. "I love seeing cool stuff!"

A few moments later, we took a taxi to the National Historical Museum in Rio De Janeiro.

"Wow!" exclaimed Valencia as we arrived at the National Historical Museum in Rio de Janeiro.

Dad told us that this museum is located in Santiago Fort and covers around twenty thousand square meters. That is ten times larger than our house in Atlanta! We were very excited to see the different collections inside the museum.

As we went inside, we were greeted by a lovely lady. She was going to be our guide for the day.

"Hello kids!" she turned to us. "My name is Maria, and I will be giving you a tour around Rio de Janeiro National Historical Museum. Are you ready?"

"Yes!" Valencia and I exclaimed in unison.

Miss Maria explained, "Before we start exploring, you should know that this fort was built in 1567. This very building was built in 1603, and it used to be a prison. The museum was not opened until 1922, and more than a decade later, it became a world-famous museum. Every day, our museum is visited by hundreds of tourists and fans of Latin American history from around the world."

She continued, "The museum owns more than 287,000 items relation to the history of Latin

Brazilian Culture Exchange

America. The library contains approximately 57,000 books, many of which have been stored here since the 15th century, and more than 50,000 historical documents and photos."

"I can't wait to explore around! Let's go!" I exclaimed, and so we started our tour around the whole museum.

First, we visited the Colonization and Dependence gallery. There, we learned about the nation's economic development through the growth and distribution of coffee in their country, as well as the mining and sugarcane industries which Dad had previously told us about. Here, our family was able to see the equipment they used on coffee plantations as well as the objects related to mining and molding of metals.

Next, we headed to the life-size replica of a 19th century pharmacy. It was very different from the ones we saw on television.

"These are amazing items!" Mom said as she took a closer look at the equipment.

"This replica of a 19th century pharmacy features the different tools and materials that they used a long time ago. As you can see, we have various scales, bowls and cutters as well as other equipment involved in making, measuring and dispensing of medicine," Miss Maria said as she pointed to the various bowls and strange-looking equipment that I'd never seen before.

After that, we went to my favorite part of the museum, the collection of carriages and automobiles. This included the light carriage used by Emperor Pedro II, who ruled Brazil for more than half a century, as Miss Maria told us. She promised to show us the emperor's throne and tell us more about him later.

"Here," Miss Maria pointed towards an old carriage that was decorated in gold and red, "we have Berlinda from the 18th century, which belonged to the Portuguese Royal Family."

"The carriage is called Berlinda?" I asked.

"Yes, Mori," replied Miss Maria.

"Then she must be a girl!" proclaimed my little sister.

"We're not sure about that…" Miss Maria smiled. At the back, I saw Mom trying to stop her laughter. We moved on to an automobile this time, which was my most favorite in the whole collection.

"This is Vehicle Protos, a 17/31 OS Landaulet model with space for six people and a wooden body. Believe it or not, this is one of the only two copies left in the world," said Miss Maria as she walked with us towards a magnificent automobile.

"That looks amazing!" Valencia and I screamed in excitement as we walked as close as we could to take a better look.

It is my first time seeing an actual car with a wooden body, because these days you only see cars made of metal and steel. It is amazing how it can carry six people without breaking! Dad and I took a closer look at the old vehicle, and we saw that it had a steering wheel like our car at home. We couldn't ride it because it has to be preserved in the museum, but I feel good by just looking at it and knowing that my ancestors probably enjoyed the comfort of cars in the past too.

"I love cars!" I exclaimed.

Maria showed us another automobile, the 1908 PROTOS, that belonged to the Brazilian diplomat, Jose Paranhos. She told us that he was the Baron of Rio Branco. We were amazed to see another car built more than a century ago.

Before moving on to the Patio of Canons, we passed by a temporary exhibit of indigenous vases. Maria told us that they won't be around for a very long time unlike the other collections in this exhibit, so we all took a closer look at them. They were huge, and made out of clay. We have a similar vase at home, where Mom keeps her beautiful plants in.

After that, we went to the Patio of Canons. Seeing real canons, like the ones in the pirate movies, felt like a dream for me. They were huge, and I think anyone who was hit by these canons would truly die! There were lots of canons to look at, with different shapes and sizes. Maria told us that the collection is a mix of English, French and Dutch canons.

Later, we proceeded to the exhibition of sacred art to continue our journey.

Brazilian Culture Exchange

THE NATIONAL MUSEUM PT. 2

We went to see the shrines, sculptures and paintings. Our family saw pictures ordered by the government to record historical events in Brazil. This included *the Consecration of Emperor D. Pedro II*, a beautiful oil painting made by Manuel de Araujo Porto Alegre.

"What is a consecration, Miss Maria?" I asked.

"Emperor Dom Pedro II was crowned and consecrated in his early life. When he ascended to the throne, Pedro II was only five years old," replied Miss Maria. "A coronation is an event where a monarch is crowned and power is transferred to the ruler. A *sacre* or consecration, on the other hand, is a religious ceremony which makes temporal or non-religious power become holy."

"Wow, Emperor Dom Pedro was our age when he became an emperor!" exclaimed Valencia.

Miss Maria added, "Dom Pedro II was nicknamed 'the Magnanimous,' which means very generous or forgiving. He was the second and last ruler of the Empire of Brazil, reigning for over fifty-eight years. His father's departure to Europe in 1831 left five-year-old Pedro II as Emperor and led to a grim and lonely childhood and adolescence."

"Why is that?" I asked.

"Unlike you kids, Dom Pedro II didn't have any time to play. He was busy studying in preparation to rule and he only had few friends. But because of that, Dom Pedro II grew into a man with a strong sense of duty and devotion toward his country and his people. He was seen as a hero, a model citizen, a caring monarch, and the source of national unity and well-being. He gained the support of the people throughout his reign, and is well-known for being an effective ruler. Because of that, many scholars rank Emperor Dom Pedro II as the greatest Brazilian," she answered.

"I want to be like Emperor Dom Pedro when I grow up!" I declared.

"Me too!" added Valencia and we high-fived.

"Then you have to study like him too, kids," said Mom with a bright smile on her face. We moved on to the next painting, with Dad following right behind us.

"This is a painting of the Naval Battle of Riachuelo, made by Victor Meirelles in 1882," Miss Maria pointed to a huge painting on the wall. There were many ships and people by the sea, who were fighting

each other.

"Why are they fighting? Why are they killing each other, Miss Maria?" asked my little sister.

"The battle of the Riachuelo on June 11 1865, was a decisive naval engagement of the Triple Alliance War which lasted from 1864 to 1870. Paraguay's marshal-president, Francisco Solano Lopez, needed to get rid of the Brazilian and Argentine ships in Parana River so he could invade northeastern Argentina. Back then Argentina, Brazil, and Uruguay were allies, while Paraguay was their enemy. In fact, Emperor Pedro II was one of the commanders of Brazil."

"Paraguay planned a surprise attack at dawn. They were delayed however, and it lost the element of surprise. Because of this, the Paraguayans proceeded to lose every chance to maneuver against the Brazilian streamers. They fought for six long hours. In the end, the Paraguayans were forced to retreat upriver. Many lives were lost on both sides, including Paraguayan admiral Ignacio Meza, who died from wounds the next day. The War of the Triple Alliance became a very important part of South American History."

After teaching us about the story behind the painting, Miss Maria led us to more sections of the

Brazilian Culture Exchange

museum. We viewed aspects of the city of Rio de Janeiro though the paintings of artist Leandro Joaquim, in the famous series known as *Ovals* because of their shape.

We also went to see the sculpture of Emperor Dom Pedro II one last time before leaving the museum. When we arrived earlier, the sculpture made by Francisco Manuel Chaves Pinheiro in 1866 welcomed us. He was riding a horse in the sculpture, and Miss Maria told us that it was also built to honor the Paraguayan War, or the War of the Triple Alliance.

We had so much fun in the museum that Valencia and I couldn't stop talking about it in the taxi on the way back to the hotel. I learned a lot about the history of South America and Brazil because of our trip today.

"Mom, can we make an oil painting at home too?" I asked Mom. "When we go to the grocery store, we buy lots of oil, right?"

"Right! Let us make a painting of our visit to the National Historical Museum in Brazil! Then we can hang it in the living room," replied Valencia in excitement.

"Calm down, kids. We can't use cooking oil to make paintings like the ones you saw in the museum, but if you guys are good, I promise we'll make paintings at home. Isn't that right, Dad?"

"Whatever you want, kids. As long as it isn't harmful, Dad will support you," replied Dad.

"This is truly the best trip ever!"

Brazilian Culture Exchange

EXCURSION IN THE AMAZON

"We're going to the Amazon!" I exclaimed.

We arrived at the Cristalino Lodge after almost a day of travelling, where we would have a once-in-a-lifetime experience. It was named by National Geographic Traveler in 2013 as one of the 25 best eco-lodges in the world! Mom and Dad booked a bungalow before we flew all the way to Brazil. After arranging some of our stuff and taking a short rest, we set out to see the different animals in the Amazon.

"Hello," a tall man approached us at the meeting point with a bright smile. "My name is Marco, and I will be your tour guide for this journey. Are you ready, kids?"

"Yes!" Valencia and I shouted at the same time. We were so excited!

"Just to give a little information about our location, Cristalino is the name of the Amazon river whose dark waters run for 114 miles, from its source in the state of Pará to its mouth in Mato Grosso, where Cristalino Lodge is located," Mister Marco explained. "The Portuguese word *cristalino* means crystal clear, which is a perfect description of this pure, well-preserved river."

"Mister Marco, didn't you say that the Amazon River has dark waters? Then how is it crystal clear?" I asked.

"The dark color of the water is caused by the tannin released from decaying leaves and pink granite rock formations, Mori. It is not caused by trash and pollution, unlike dirty streams in the city."

Mister Marco continued sharing information with us about the place as we walked towards the observation tower. We were told that the observation tower would enable us to see some of the Amazon's beautiful animals from above, as if we were one of the birds. Because the trees around us are 25-45 meters tall, we had to climb up a 50-meter tall tower. Although it was a little tiring, the whole process was really safe and the view from above was spectacular!

"Dad, are you alright?" I held Dad's hand, sensing that he was nervous as soon as we reached the top. Valencia and Mom also stood by his side.

"We're always so high up in the air!" he complained. "Still, I have to admit that the view is breathtaking."

"We won't be able to see such landscapes anywhere else," replied Mom.

We used the telescope that Mister Marco carried around to observe the beauty of nature even more. There were so many trees! Looking intently, we saw lots of birds, like macaws, parakeets, parrots, tanagers and cotingas.

Not only that, but we saw some monkeys as well. Among them was the white-whiskered spider monkey. It is called that because from afar, it looks like a big spider. The monkey has long, spider-like limbs and the fur covering its body is black, except for a white patch on its forehead and a white line between the ears and chin.

We were also able to see the white-nosed saki monkey. It has black fur covering its whole body as well, except for its nose which Valencia and I find really cute. Unfortunately, both of these monkey species are endangered and need to be protected.

After an amazing experience at the watchtower, we went on a hiking trip to the forest to see more animals up close. Valencia and I followed Mom and Dad's instructions, as well as Mister Marco's, so that we could have a safe journey.

Brazilian Culture Exchange

Our family was able to witness the Brazilian tapir, which is the largest land mammal in South America. The white-lipped and collared peccary, and capybara also welcomed us. Mister Marco said that these large animals feed mainly on plants and roots, and are able to move quickly through the forest.

"T-that's..." Valencia stuttered, her legs shaking in fear as she pointed towards the Brazilian tapir facing our way. I wanted it to come closer so that we could take a better look and say hi, but my little sister felt the opposite.

Mister Marco assured that the Brazilian tapir wouldn't come anywhere near us, and that it probably just wanted to say hello. Valencia was still scared after hearing that, and I thought she'd cry! Because of that, Dad decided to carry her to ease her nervousness.

Dad didn't want Valencia to miss the beauty of the rest of the forest, and in that very moment, I knew that I wanted to be a hero like Dad. Not even a minute later, Valencia calmed down and she rested her head on Dad's shoulder. Our tour carried on, and Mom held my left hand as we walked a little deeper into the forest.

Brazilian Culture Exchange

We were able to see different butterflies and moths. Mister Marco said that the Cristalino area contains around two thousand species of butterflies and moths, so they are impossible to miss. We saw even more birds, and we came to witness the rufous-capped Nunlet, which can only be found in Bolivia, Brazil and Peru. Additionally, we saw some cuckoos.

We walked around three hours at a regular pace, but I could not feel myself getting tired. Valencia smiled from ear to ear now, and Mom and Dad made sure that we were safe. There was so much to see, with thousands of different plants and animals in the area. Sure, we couldn't get the chance to observe all of them, but we saw species we've never seen before which is exactly how I dreamt this trip would be! Soon, we conquered the trail tour and headed back to the bungalow.

Taking a rest after our wonderful trip, we went to our private bungalow and stayed on the veranda to enjoy the view. Valencia and I were having fun swinging on the hammock while Mom and Dad watched us, enjoying their coffee.

"When you're much older, let us come back and go canoeing," suggested Dad.

"That's right. We can go in pairs, that would be so

much fun!" replied Mom with a bright smile on her face.

"What's canoeing?" I asked.

"You'll get the chance to row a boat with me, or your Mom," replied Dad. "We can have a race!"

"But we can only go when you're much older, to ensure your safety," added Mom.

Valencia asked, "So we can row a boat?"

"Just a small boat," replied Dad.

"I will work hard to grow up faster so we can come back soon!" I exclaimed, making Mom and Dad laugh.

At that moment, I felt very happy to be traveling around the world with my family. I wouldn't trade this precious memory for anything else, and I will remember it for the rest of my life.

Brazilian Culture Exchange

FESTIVAL!

A few days after our trip to the Amazon, we were back in Rio de Janeiro, just in time to catch the Samba Parade that is held to celebrate the Rio Carnival. From what we heard, visitors from around the world come to Rio for a week of dancing, singing and partying. Today, we were lucky enough to be one of the seventy-thousand spectators to watch the show here in the Sambadrome. Mom said that the parade has been held here since 1984.

"When is it going to start?" complained Valencia. I just laughed and shared a cookie with her. Meanwhile, Dad was getting ready with the camera to take pictures of the parade.

"It will start soon," replied Mom. "Each year, twelve of the top samba schools compete for the prestigious championship title."

"They are having a contest?" I asked.

She said, "Yes, Mori. We are fortunate enough to see their stunning performances today."

"Unlike street events where people move however they want, the shows you will see are highly choreographed despite the very large scale of the performance," added Dad. "This is the reason why we agreed to bring you here, because it is completely safe for us to watch."

"Oh, it's starting!"

Soon, a loud bang spread all over the dome's atmosphere. Everyone in their seats were excited. Finally, thousands of dancers entered the stage and the music provided the rhythm for them to dance to.

All of the dancers wore colorful costumes, and some of them looked like they were wearing wings on their backs! The first performance's theme was Egypt, and everyone was lavishly dressed in gold and black. All of them danced samba beautifully.

Soon, large floats emerged. There were floats depicting the pharaohs and the pyramids, and one float that caught our interest was Vila Isabel's float, with a golden human pyramid. The lady on top of the float wore wings with white and orange feathers.

Dad commented, "Not only are their dancing and choreography skills impressive, but also the massive effort they put into making these floats."

Everyone in the crowd enjoyed the show, tapping to the beat of the drums that roared throughout the

dome. People cheered for the schools that they supported, while I pointed out my favorites to Mom. She said that the costumes and floats were secretly created by the locals inside their communities, only to be revealed on the day of the performance. Each show was so impressive! They must have practiced for months.

"This is not an easy show to pull off, kids. It takes determination and creativity," said Mom. "Many people help in making the performance possible, and teamwork is very valuable. They take on roles, and no role is too small or large: everyone is important."

"What roles?" asked Valencia.

"From what I heard, they are divided into groups. Of course, the Carnival Designer, known as the 'Carnavalesco,' takes on a big part in designing and directing the whole show," explained Mom.

"There are groups like 'The Wings' or the 'Alas' of the parade composed of between twenty and one hundred people who wear a particular costume and perform the same role, 'The Front Commission,' also known as the 'Vanguard Commission,' that opens the school's parade and provides the first impression for the audience and judges, and 'The Passistas' who are amongst the best dancers of the school. These groups come together to bring a lively performance and pride to their alma mater. They perform their hearts out for our entertainment, in order not to let down their institution and the communities supporting them.

"There are also notable individuals throughout the whole routine, like the 'Queen of the Samba School' who leads the procession, and the 'Godmother' who has been with the school for a long period of time. Additionally, there are eight to ten floats which are highly decorated according to the theme and often carry special guests."

I commented, "Wow, getting everything right must be really hard."

"I want to learn how to dance samba like them so I can wear beautiful costumes like the Queen!" exclaimed Valencia.

We watched the colorful performances of twelve schools in glee. Each of them had different themes, like butterflies, and even monkeys! Moments later, the judges crowned this year's champion, and the whole dome cheered for them. We took pictures with some of the performers before going back to the hotel after a long but beautiful day.

A NIGHT TO REMEMBER

"Dad," I tugged on Dad's shirt as he combed his hair after taking a bath. "Are we going to stay in Brazil forever?"

"No son," answered Dad. "We are actually flying back home on tomorrow."

"But I am not ready to go yet…" I said with a frown. I couldn't believe that we were going home tomorrow, when we'd had so much fun this past week.

"That's right, Dad. I want to go back to the Amazon to see some more animals," said Valencia.

"Alright kids, since this is our last day… let's go and enjoy a family dinner at Fogo de Chao," replied Mom.

"Mom, what's Fogo de Chao?" asked Valencia.

"Fogo de Chao is a Brazilian steakhouse where you can eat a variety of meat as well as different kinds of steak," answered Mom. "The restaurant is located by Sugarloaf Mountain which should be enjoyable!"

"Mom, I love sugar!" stated Valencia. "I can't wait to go."

"Dad, why are you smiling?" asked Mori.

"All-you-can-eat meat selections are my favorite and I can't wait to eat filet mignon," replied Dad.

"Dad, I can't wait to eat my sugar steak too!" stated Valencia.

"Valencia, there is no such thing as sugar steak!" I said as I burst into laughter. Valencia frowned, so I apologized to my little sister for making fun of her. Instead, Mom explained why it is impossible to make a sugar steak.

"Okay children, that's enough. Change your clothes now, we'll be leaving in ten minutes," said Mom.

"Where are we going, Mom?" I asked.

"You will see," replied Mom.

I ran to the closet, taking the first shirt and pair of pants that I could find. I wasn't going to let our last day be wasted and I will enjoy every single moment we have left in Brazil. When we go home, I will tell my friends all about our trip!

Several minutes later, we left the hotel and rode a taxi to Mom's secret destination. As soon as we arrived, Valencia and I were impressed by the amazing architecture. Immediately, I recognized where we were: a shopping mall!

"We're here in Shopping Nova America to buy items that you would like to bring home as a remembrance of our trip, and to buy souvenirs for our loved ones and friends back at home. Are you ready, kids?" asked Mom.

Brazilian Culture Exchange

"Can we go to the arcade later?" I replied.

"Let's do everything you want to do on our last day, kids!" exclaimed Dad and we started our shopping adventure immediately.

First, we went to a boutique called Josefina Rosa Cor with Mom. Dad and I waited for Valencia and Mom outside the boutique while they chose bags for Mom and her friends. In the end, Mom bought a large leather tote bag for herself and a couple of handbags for her friends.

After that, we went to a jewelry store called Monte Carlo. Mom said that Grandma wanted us to buy a necklace for her as a souvenir of our trip in Brazil. Dad chose a silver necklace with a clear, blue topaz pendant for Grandma. He said that Grandma would like the light color, which will remind her of the Brazilian seas. Mom and Dad paid for the necklace before we headed to our next shop, called Kings.

It was time for me and Dad to look around, while Valencia and Mom waited outside. There were loads of stuff to choose from, like shirts and caps. Dad bought a messenger bag for himself, and I bought black cap for me and a red cap for Valencia. I didn't tell her about it, so that it could be a surprise when we unpack our luggage at home.

Later on, we entered a large clothing shop called South. Here, we picked shirts for our close relatives and friends that will remind them of us and of

Brazil. There were shirts with various prints, some displaying the beauty of the tourist spots of Rio de Janeiro like the Christ the Redeemer shirt, and some shirts with large "Rio de Janeiro" prints on them with tropical designs.

Mom also shopped for blouses with colorful patterns, depicting the bright and lively culture of Brazil. She and Valencia tried a few of them on, and they looked absolutely stunning. Mom and Dad paid for over a dozen shirts and tops, both for us and for the people back home.

A few shopping bags later, we finally finished getting everything we needed. Shopping with my family was a fun experience, and so lunch came pretty quickly. We stopped by the food court to get some food. What I liked about it was the wide variety of food available, and that we could still sit together and eat at one table despite getting food from different kiosks. Because we have different tastes in food, the food court is the best and quickest option for us.

Having finished our meal, Mom and Dad agreed to buy us some ice cream for dessert. We came across Los Paleteros and they offered popsicle ice cream in different flavors, some we have never tasted before.

Mom ordered the Maracuja with condensed milk flavor, while I tried their Brigadeiro flavored ice cream. The saleslady told us that this ice cream flavor was inspired by a Brazilian delicacy called Brigadeiro, which was more or less similar to chocolate cake pops covered with different toppings. Mom made a reminder in her phone to buy actual Brigadeiros before going home. Dad tried the Jamaican flavored ice cream while Valencia chose strawberry shortcake. We were satisfied by the extremely delicious dessert and went straight to the arcade after drinking some water to clear our throats.

Valencia and I enjoyed a few games with Mom and Dad in the arcade. Dad and I played a shooter game, and we were shooting zombies like superheroes! Dad shot almost all of the zombies that approached me, and if not for him, I would have been killed in the game quickly! We reached the final stage and conquered the last battle together. Dad and I make a great team of soldiers! Valencia played a toy crane with Mom, and they won a couple of stuffed toys. We enjoyed roaming around for an hour before heading back to the hotel to get some rest before heading to Fogo de Chao.

Back in the hotel, Valencia and I helped Mom and Dad organize everything we bought from Shopping Nova America. After that, I took a shower to freshen up and watched the Brazilian cartoon series that my little sister and I came to like while we stayed here. It was our last day here, so we should enjoy every moment we had left.

Valencia and I took a short nap to recharge ourselves, while Mom and Dad enjoyed coffee on the balcony. A couple of hours later, they woke us up to prepare for our dinner by Sugarloaf Mountain.

As soon as we were ready, we then left the hotel to see the Sugarloaf Mountain and eat a delicious Brazilian meal for the last time.

When we arrived, we were greeted by the magnificent view of city lights, and most of all, the Sugarloaf Mountain. There was light coming from below the mountain, and you could still see the rock formation from afar. Botafogo Bay was beautiful, and the restaurant was packed with guests. The moment we stepped foot inside the restaurant, a waiter led us to the table that Mom and Dad had reserved.

As soon as we were settled, Dad, Valencia, and I ran to the buffet table. Mom followed closely behind, laughing at how excited we were. There was just the best reason to be excited: all-you-can-eat food!

There was a really wide variety of meat to choose from, and Dad got a piece of everything except for his filet mignon, which I remember to be one whole plate. All of the selections were mouthwatering! And of course, we couldn't forget the mashed potatoes, could we?

Mom went to the salad bar, which offered a fresh variety of vegetables and fruits, as well as seasonings. I even remember an area dedicated to cheese... and I love cheese! There were all kinds of cheese, like blue cheese, mozzarella, parmesan, everything I could think of!

Brazilian Culture Exchange

Valencia and I picked a small portion of everything, filling our plates. Of course, Mom and Dad told us to be careful, and that we shouldn't take more than we could eat to prevent food from going to waste. I picked some salami, bread, and cheese before heading back to our table.

I considered myself very lucky to be eating this delicious steak right then, when children on the other side of the world had almost nothing to eat. I made sure to savor the taste of the steak, but my thoughts were interrupted by Valencia's words.

"Ahh! Dad's steak is still raw on the inside! I hate the taste of blood!" she squealed, pointing at Dad's medium rare steak.

"Valencia, I am sure you'll come to like it when you're older," answered Dad. "Medium rare is the best way to cook steak."

"Why don't you have a bite of salad, dear?" asked Mom as she offered a spoonful to my little sister. As soon as the food entered her mouth, she smiled almost instantly.

"Mom, your salad is delicious!" exclaimed Valencia. "There's some sweetness in it."

"You really have weird tastes, little sister," I said. "I wouldn't trade steak for salad!"

Dad laughed, giving me a large portion of filet mignon. The moment I took a bite, I instantly fell in love. It was juicy, tender and everything I imagined it to be. Paired with some mashed potatoes, my whole mouth had a party going on inside! It was amazing.

More than the food, we were treated to a beautiful view by the bay as we ate. Glancing at the other guests, they were all very happy to be with their friends and families, and smiles were evident on their faces. Because of that, I realized one thing.

"Mom, I just realized something."

"What is it, Mori?" asked Mom.

"I think that the taste of food is important, but who you are eating the food with is the most important thing of all," I answered with pride, and Dad gave me a soft pat on the shoulder.

He added, "That's right, son. It doesn't matter if you're eating a one-dollar budget meal, or a thousand-dollar five course meal. What matters is the people you get to share this blessing with, and whether or not you are happy with their company."

"I am very proud of you, Mori," replied Mom.

Throughout the meal, we talked about our whole journey here in Brazil. I remember how Dad and I had to rush to the restroom ten minutes before our flight because I was too excited and I had to pee. That was really funny!

When we arrived at Rio Othon Palace, it felt as if we

Brazilian Culture Exchange

were the royal family, and our castle by the sea was waiting for us. It was everything I imagined, and the lazy afternoon on Copacabana beach was super relaxing after a long flight.

We went to see *Christ the Redeemer* up close, and defied gravity by conquering Sugarloaf Mountain. I can still remember how scared Dad was when we first got there, but he got rid of all of his fears for me and Valencia, and we enjoyed our trip. He's the best Dad we could ever ask for!

Additionally, we talked about our trip to the National Historical Museum. *A journey to a different country will never be complete without knowing its history and culture,* Mom once said. We discovered lots of things and came to love this country even more for their heritage. The architecture was also amazing!

During our trip, one of my biggest dreams was fulfilled. We went to the Amazon to interact with the wild animals up close, and we were able to see all of the birds and animals in the air like we were flying! I will never forget that experience in Cristalino Lodge, and I will definitely come back when I'm older so that we can go canoeing.

Last but not least, we went to enjoy the Rio Samba Parade, which helped our family appreciate Brazilian culture even more. I cannot forget the colorful costumes, the wonderful dances, and the cheers of the people who enjoyed the show. Our trip may come to an end, but the memories will never fade away. This is a trip I will never forget.

"Mori, what is the biggest lesson you've learned throughout our trip?" asked Mom.

"The biggest lesson I've learned is to be open and embrace other cultures and learn from them. I really enjoyed our stay here, and it would not be possible without the people who welcomed us to their country," I answered. "I also learned that Dad will conquer all of his fears just for us!"

"That's right, kids!" exclaimed Dad as he smiled proudly.

"That is so heartwarming, Mori. You sound wiser than your age, dear," said Mom. "What about you, Valencia?"

"I learned that we should take good care of the animals around us, and we should pay more attention to Mother Earth's call for help,'" answered Valencia with glee. "When we went to the Amazon, I learned that there are more endangered animals than I expected, and we should take care of them!"

"That is right, Valencia. We are not the only creatures living on this Earth, so we should take care of it," replied Mom.

"Also, I rediscovered my love for sweets in Brazil, Mom!" she exclaimed.

"It's good to eat sweets occasionally dear, but don't

eat them too often or you can damage your teeth," replied Mom. "We can make desserts at home with natural sweeteners, if you would like. They are healthier options compared to sugar."

"As long as it's sweet!" stated Valencia. Dad and I agreed to Mom's idea.

We stayed a little longer, enjoying the view and each other's company. Before leaving, we took a lot of pictures to include in our photo album. I even took a picture with a steak that was bigger than my head! It was a hilarious photo.

We rode a taxi back to the hotel and went to sleep early to prepare for our flight the next morning. This time, Mom and Dad made sure to set the alarm correctly before going to bed.

"Big brother, where do you want to go next?" asked Valencia. We were lying in bed with Mom and Dad.

"I haven't thought about it yet. How about you? Where do you want to go?" I replied.

"I don't know either. What about you, Mom?" Valencia turned to Mom, who was just about to turn off her cellphone.

"I'm fine with going anywhere, as long as it is with you and your father. Our family is the most important treasure to me," replied Mom.

"What about you, Dad? Where do you want to go

next?" I asked Dad.

"Somewhere with less tourist spots that are high above the ground, please," joked Dad. "Just kidding, kids. Dad will go wherever you want to go, as long as your Mom allows it."

"Mom, Dad, Valencia… this is the best trip ever!" I whispered, leaving a kiss on their cheeks before closing my eyes and going to sleep.

Now that our trip is over, I can't wait to tell everyone at home about our Brazilian journey!

ABOUT THE AUTHOR

GEISZEL GODOY Married to Manuel Godoy, Geiszel joined the writing game in August of 2017 by creating Mori's Family Adventures. Her focus on traditional families and organization has brought her extreme success in the genre.

"The family unit is untapped in today's society because everyone wants to entertain either the child or the parent. Why can't we do both and educate them as well?"

Made in the USA
Columbia, SC
21 June 2018